A is for At Bat

A BASEBALL PRIMER

Illustrations by Andy Nelson
Rhymes by Ken LaZebnik and Steve Lehman

Culpepper Press
SIREN • MINNEAPOLIS

*To our parents,
who gave us a love of baseball
and, more important, a
love of reading*

Aa

A is for at bat.
You step up to the plate.
The pitch is a fastball,
Which makes you swing late.

Bb

B is for bullpen,
Where pitchers aspire
To get in the game
If the starter should tire.

Cc

C is for coach.
He'll give you a sign:
To take, swing away,
Or bunt down the line.

Dd

D is for dugout,
That hole in the stands
Where players not playing
Must sit on their hands.

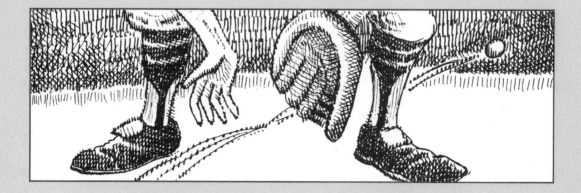

Ee

E is for E-6,
Error: shortstop.
He had it, he thought,
But it took a bad hop.

Ff

F is for foul ball.
You hit it and then
The ump calls, "Time Out!"
You must try it again.

Gg

G is for goose eggs.
A run can't be bought:
We're now in the ninth
And it's nothing to naught.

Hh

H is for homer.
The Sultan of Swat
Hit 714
Before Aaron got hot.

Ii

I is for infield,
The old double play:
Tinker to Evers to Chance—
Two away.

Jj

J is for jammed,
A hard one in tight,
To move you away
From the plate for the night.

Kk

K is for strike-out,
But don't ask me why.
You miss it three times,
You don't get a fourth try.

Ll

L is for lefty,
Like Carlton and Spahn
And Koufax and Gomez
But not Drysdale, Don.

Mm

M is for mask,
Keeping foul tips at bay,
But on pop-ups at home
Catchers throw it away.

Nn

N is for the natural.
Scouting is done:
He'll hit, hit for power,
Can throw well and run.

Oo

O is for on deck.
You watch and you wait.
When the batter is done
You'll step up to the plate.

Pp

P is for pitchout;
The runner might go.
This pitch helps the catcher
To make a good throw.

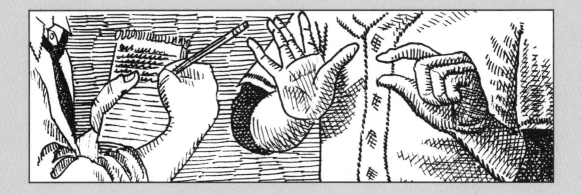

Qq

Q is for questions.
Reporters must ask
The players some tough ones,
For that is their task.

Rr

R is rounding third,
They're waving him in,
The throw's to the plate—
If he makes it, we win!

Ss

S is for spitball,
Covered with drool.
This is a pitch
They don't teach you at school.

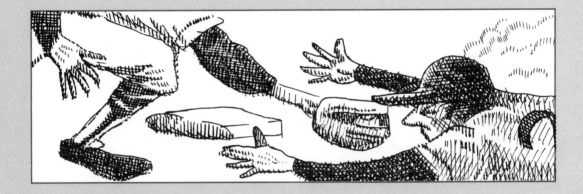

Tt

T is for tag.
He slides toward the base,
But the glove with the ball
Stares him right in the face.

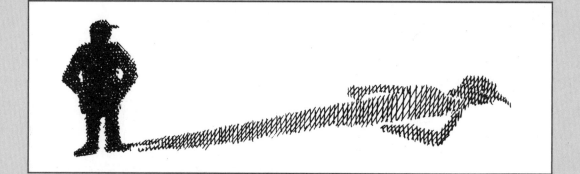

Uu

U is for ump.
You may think he's a bum,
But argue too much
And he'll give you the thumb.

Vv

V is for vines
On the Wrigley Field wall.
If you hit it out there,
They may swallow the ball.

Ww

W stands
For the warning track dirt,
It says, "Don't run into
The wall and get hurt!"

Xx

X is for ex,
As in ex-baseball great.
At old-timers' games
He'll return to the plate.

Yy

Y is for "Yer out!"
The ump roars in high style.
"Are you blind? Can't you see?
I was safe by a mile!"

Zz

Z is for bench warmers
Sleeping away.
They got a bit drowsy
While waiting to play.

Glossary

Carlton, Steve. Also known as Lefty. Famed lefthanded pitcher of the Sixties, Seventies and Eighties.

Drysdale, Don. Hall of Fame righthanded pitcher, a teammate of Sandy Koufax.

E-6. Scoring is a shorthand method of recording the events of a baseball game. In this shorthand, each defensive player is assigned a number so that his involvement in handling the ball during a play may be easily chronicled. E signifies error. Number six is the shortstop. Hence, E-6 means that the batter or runner advanced due to the shortstop's misplay.

Gomez, Lefty. Hall of Fame left-handed pitcher of the Thirties and Forties.

Jammed refers to a fastball inside, or near the batter, thrown with the intent of either causing the batter to hit the ball weakly off the handle part of the bat or forcing him to stand a bit farther away from the plate next time, putting him at a disadvantage on outside pitches.

K is the scoring symbol for strikeout, perhaps deriving from boxing's term *KO* (knock out). It is used to distinguish a strikeout (K) from a single (S). (See E-6 for more information about scoring.)

Koufax, Sandy. Hall of Fame left-handed pitcher of the Fifties and Sixties.

Spahn, Warren. Hall of Fame left-handed pitcher of the Forties, Fifties and Sixties.

Sultan of Swat. One of several nicknames for George Herman (Babe) Ruth. The Bambino, as he was also known, was one of the greatest hitters of all time. His records for most home runs in a season and most home runs in a career stood for over thirty years. The latter record, 714, was surpassed in 1974 by Henry (Hammerin' Hank) Aaron.

Take. A signal from the third base coach to the batter instructing him to refrain from swinging at the next pitch. Conversely, the sign to swing away would free the batter to try to hit the next pitch offered.

Tinker to Evers to Chance. Joe Tinker, shortstop, Johnny Evers, second baseman, and Frank Chance, first baseman, formed a legendary double play combination for the Chicago Cubs during the early years of this century. Their prowess was immortalized in the poem *Baseball's Sad Lexicon* by Franklin P. Adams in 1908. Adams, a New York Giants fan, bemoaned the tendency of the three to create double plays against his team. Thus the opening line of the poem: "These are the saddest of possible words, / Tinker-to-Evers-to-Chance."

Thumb. Being given the thumb is a euphemism for being ejected from the game, usually for contesting the ruling of an umpire too vociferously.

Wrigley Field. Home of the Chicago Cubs, Wrigley Field is one of the oldest and most picturesque ballparks in the Major Leagues. It is the only big league park with ivy covering the outfield wall.